All About MARVELOUS ME!

A Draw and Write Journal

Becky J. Radtke

DOVER PUBLICATIONS, INC.
Mineola, New York

Dozens of activity pages in this one-of-a-kind book will give you a chance to tell about just how marvelous you are! You'll get to draw pictures, tell about your family and friends, describe your life up to the present time, and even write down your ideas and plans for the future. Design your "Ultimate Hangout" room, list your favorite TV shows and characters, fill in an Exercise Chart, and make up your own "Recipe for Happiness," and much more. Use your imagination to fill out each page—and you can color in the pages when you're finished!

Bibliographical Note
All About Marvelous Me! A Draw and Write Journal is a new work, first published by Dover Publications, Inc., in 2014.

International Standard Book Number
, *ISBN-13: 978-0-486-78626-1*
ISBN-10: 0-486-78626-9

Manufactured in the United States by LSC Communications
78626905   2017
www.doverpublications.com

All About Marvelous Me!

Nice to meet you!

Here's a picture of Me!

Name

Date

Let's get started!

Hooray!

Home Sweet Home

Here's a Picture of My Home

My Address is: _____
_____

My Phone Number is: _____

I have lived here for ____ years, ____ months, and ____ days.

I live here with _____
_____.

The best thing about living here is _____
_____.

Baby Beginnings

My full name is...

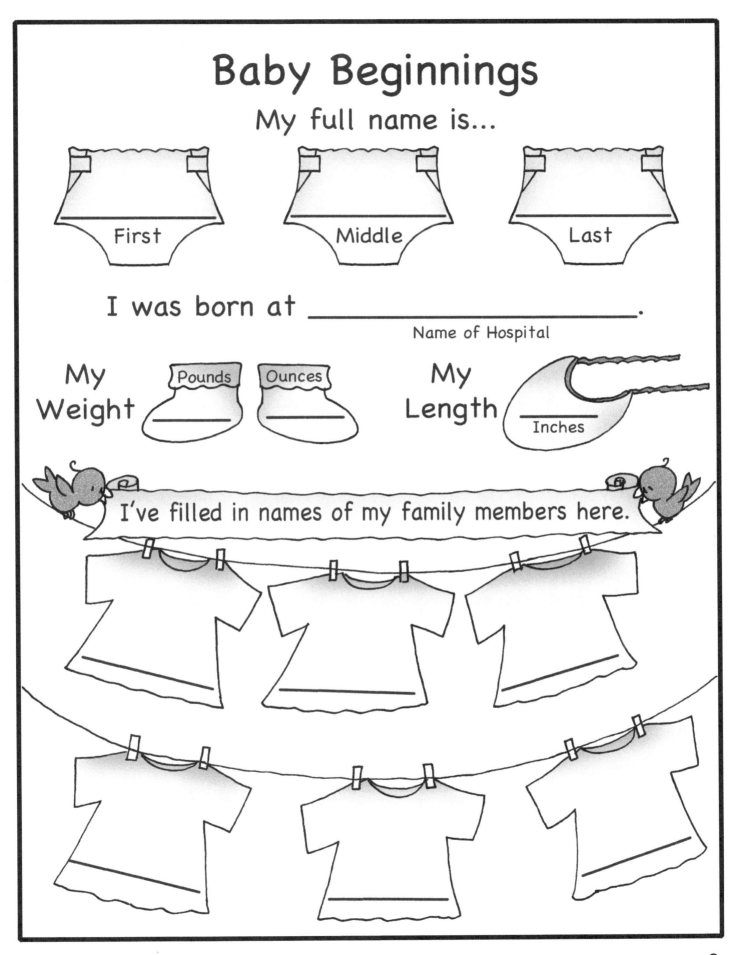

First

Middle

Last

I was born at _____.

Name of Hospital

My Weight

Pounds   Ounces

My Length

Inches

I've filled in names of my family members here.

Baby Behavior

I've circled some words that people have used to describe Me as a baby. (And added 3 more!)

Happy	Active	
Fussy	_____	Quiet
Determined	_____	Funny
Loud	_____	Sleepy
Contented	Independent	Sensitive

My Very Important Person

Someone who plays a big part in my life is

_____.

A picture of my V.I.P.!

Some wonderful qualities this person has are:

_____

_____

More V. I. P. S

Three more people who mean a lot to Me!

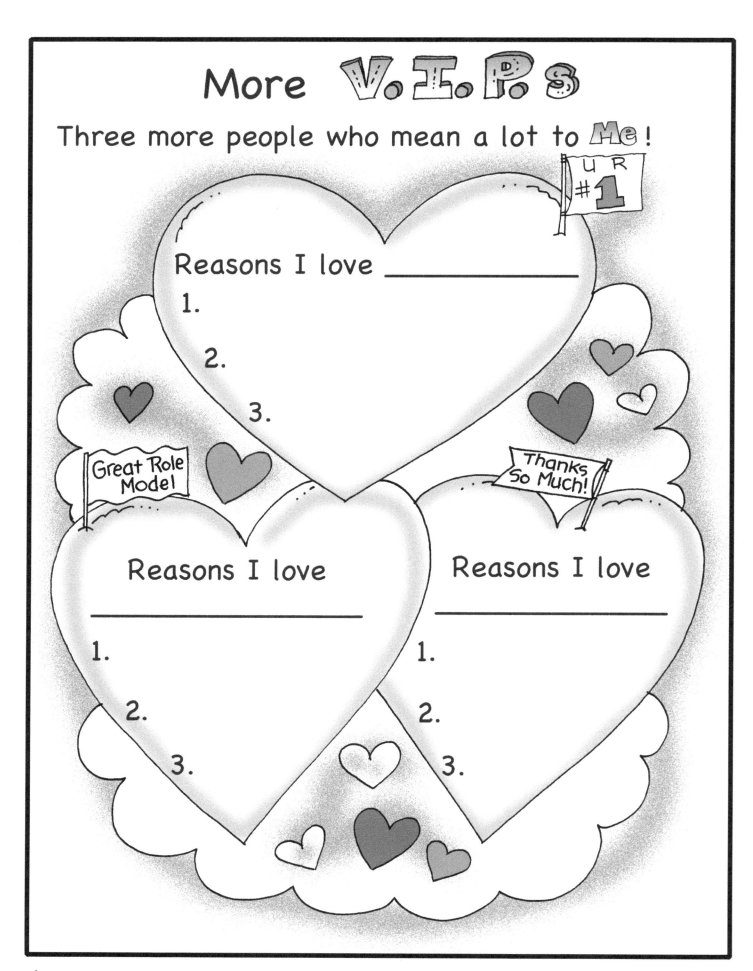

Reasons I love _____

1.

2.

3.

Reasons I love

_____

1.

2.

3.

Reasons I love

_____

1.

2.

3.

Great Role Model

Thanks So Much!

U R #1

Family and Friends Tree

Here are names and pictures of some of my family and friends.

Personality Plus

I've put a check mark by all of the words that can be used to describe Me! I'm a great blend!

- ☐ Adventurous
- ☐ Observant
- ☐ Competitive
- ☐ Imaginative
- ☐ Responsible
- ☐ Confident
- ☐ Outgoing
- ☐ Charming
- ☐ Helpful
- ☐ Intense

- ☐ Curious
- ☐ Deep Thinker
- ☐ Loyal
- ☐ Shy

Other Words
- ☐ _____
- ☐ _____
- ☐ _____

The flavor smoothie that best describes me is _____.

Mirror, Mirror

Here's a drawing of what I look like now at age ____ !

School Days

The name of my school is
_____.
The school day begins at
_____ A.M.
The school day ends at
_____ P.M.

My teacher is
_____,
grade ____.

There are ____ kids in my class.

Some of my subjects are...

I put a star by the one I'm best at!

_____
_____
_____
_____

The part of the school day I enjoy the most is...

_____
_____

Here's how I feel about going to school...

_____
_____

Lunchtime Pals

Here's a drawing of **Me** eating lunch with my friends.

Here's my lunch.

Things we talk about...

Lunch starts at...

Lunch ends at...

My Day in the City

I went to the city of

_____

with

_____.

I've drawn the faces of people in the crowd.

Here's what I thought about the city...

_____

_____

_____

My Day in the Country

I went to the
town of

_____

with

_____ .

I've circled some of the animals I got to see.

Here's what I thought about the country...

_____

_____

_____

Ice Cream Inventor

I've checked off my five favorite ice cream flavors.

- [ ] Butter Pecan
- [ ] Brownie
- [ ] Vanilla
- [ ] Chocolate Chip
- [ ] Birthday Cake
- [ ] English Toffee
- [ ] Butter Brickle
- [ ] Cotton Candy

- [ ] Peach
- [ ] Apple Pie
- [ ] Banana
- [ ] Pineapple
- [ ] Chocolate
- [ ] Pumpkin Pie
- [ ] Raspberry
- [ ] Maple Nut

- [ ] Mint Chocolate Chip
- [ ] Blueberry Cheesecake
- [ ] Cookie Dough
- [ ] S'more
- [ ] Strawberry
- [ ] Peanut Butter Cup
- [ ] _____
- [ ] _____

I've colored the scoops to look like my picks!

My idea for a new ice cream flavor is _____.

Here is the name of my new ice cream flavor! →

_____

NEW!

All the Rage

Here are some of this year's current trends.

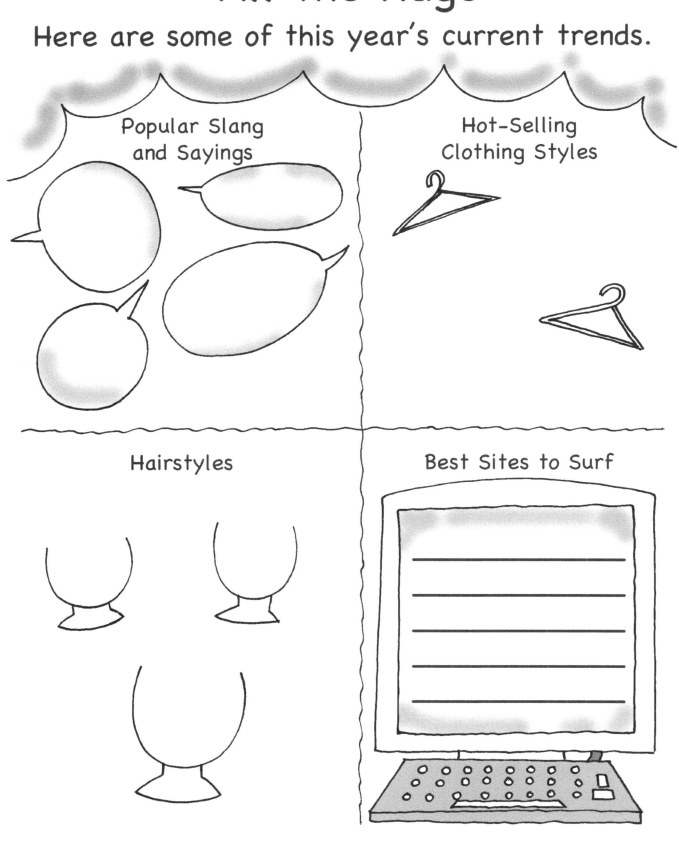

Popular Slang
and Sayings

Hot-Selling
Clothing Styles

Hairstyles

Best Sites to Surf

Someday

Take a peek! Here are some dream occupations...

Veterinarian

Police Officer

Lawyer

Writer

Chef

My → Idea

Dentist

Nurse

Carpenter

Artist

My Idea

Nurse

Teacher

Astronaut

Actor

Fire Fighter

Zoo-keeper

Here are some steps I can take to make my dream come true.

1. _____

2. _____

3. _____

Genuine Genie

If I had a genie, I would ask for these 3 things.

Wish 1

_____
_____
_____
_____

Wish 2

_____
_____
_____
_____

Wish 3

_____
_____
_____
_____

Great Times

Here are some of the best experiences
I've had...

What Happened:_____

_____

_____

_____

_____

It was awesome!

I rate it?
☐ Great
☐ Fantastic
☐ Over the Top

What Happened:_____

_____

_____

_____

_____

It was super!

I rate it?
☐ Great
☐ Fantastic
☐ Over the Top

What Happened:_____

_____

_____

_____

_____

It was sweet!

I rate it?
☐ Great
☐ Fantastic
☐ Over the Top

Presto-Change-O

Here are things I'd magically change if I could!

Abracadabra!

One _____

Two _____

Three _____

Four _____

Here's what I can really do to make one of these things happen:

_____

Best Friends Forever
My very BFF in the world is...

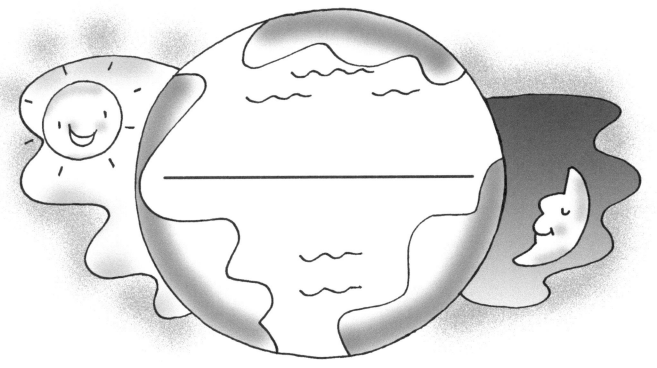

_____

We met when _____
_____.

We like to _____
_____.

This friend brightens my day by just _____
_____.

I think we will always be close because _____
_____.

Other Close Friends

I really enjoy hanging out with these friends...

_____→We met at _____
_____→We met at _____
_____→We met at _____

They are fun to be with because: _____
_____
_____

Things we like to do when we're all together:

_____
_____
_____

Friends are Awesome!

My Pets

_____
Name

is a _____.

I love my pet because:

_____

_____

_____

_____

Here's a picture of my pet!

_____
Name

is a _____.

I love my pet because:

_____

_____

_____

_____

Here's a picture of my pet!

23

Animal Adventure

If I could be any animal for one day I'd be a

_____.

I think it would be cool because I'd get to

_____.

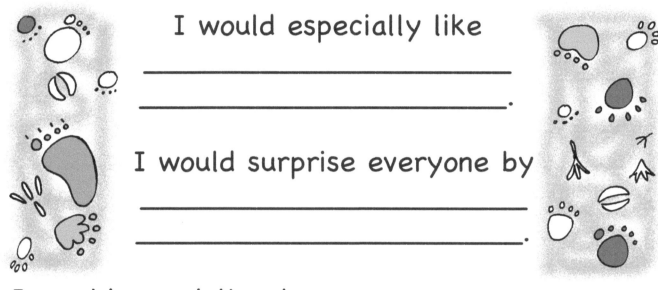

I would especially like

_____

_____.

I would surprise everyone by

_____

_____.

I would spend the day... _____

_____

_____

Pick a Planet

If I could go to any planet I would pick

_____.

It would be an interesting place to travel
to because... _____

_____

_____

I imagine my visit there would be... _____

_____

_____

Here's my drawing of an alien that I might meet there.

Welcome!

Dreamland

My dreaming habits...

I dream... ☐ Every night ☐ Often ☐ Hardly ever

I dream... ☐ Mostly good stuff ☐ Mostly bad stuff

When I dream I can remember...

☐ The whole thing ☐ Parts ☐ Not much at all

The Best Dream I've Had: _____

_____

_____

_____

_____

_____

_____

_____

How wonderful!

The Worst Dream I've Had:

_____

_____

_____

_____

_____

Spooky!

EEEK!

Invisible Me

If I could be invisible for a day, here's what I would do...

First _____

_____

_____

Then _____

_____

_____

Finally _____

_____

_____

Now you see me...

Poof

Now you don't!

Where'd he go?

The next day I would...

☐ Tell just one person what happened!

☐ Tell no one-keep it a secret.

☐ Tell all my friends!

☐ Give an interview on national television!

Birthday Wishes

Don't forget candles!

I've decorated my cake!

I drew what I most want for a gift in here!

Here are the guests I'd invite to my party:

_____

_____

_____

Scary, Scary

Things that frighten Me!

I've circled things that I find creepy...

Spiders   Snakes

Cemeteries

Old, Empty Houses

Worms

Lizards

All Bugs

Dark Forests

I've drawn one of them!

Sounds that really annoy Me!

Sirens

Scratching

Thunder

Growling

Hissing

Popping   Barking   Fireworks

MORE things that freak Me out!

_____

_____

_____

_____

_____

_____

_____

Ultimate Hangout

Here's how I would design and furnish a special room for my friends and Me!

Here are some ideas! How about a . . .

Movie Screen?

Swimming Pool?

Telescope?

Comfy Couch?

Soda/ Snack Machine?

Gaming System?

Giant Aquarium?

Best Holiday

My favorite holiday of the year is

_____!

Because...

_____

_____

_____

_____

Where we celebrate:

_____

_____

Things we do to celebrate:

_____

_____

_____

What I most look forward to:

_____

_____

_____

_____

Sport Spot

My favorite sport is _____.

My favorite player is _____.

I'm a forever fan because _____

_____

_____.

The most memorable game I watched was

_____

_____.

I've drawn my favorite team's mascot!
↓

Here's Me wearing my team's shirt!

Go Team

#1

Meow!

Snacks I enjoy while watching my team:

_____

_____

_____

_____

_____

Yum Yums

Hooray for Hobbies

My favorite hobby is

_____

_____ .

I started it because

_____

_____ .

I've been doing this for

years	months	days

I find it fun because

_____

_____

_____ .

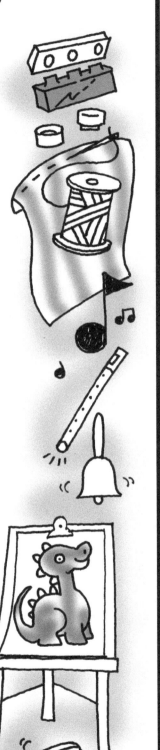

Other hobbies I'd like
to try are _____

_____

_____

_____ .

My Skills

Some things I'm good at are:

Room for Improvement

Some things that are hard for me to do are:

_____
_____
_____
_____
_____

I think I can do better if _____
_____
_____
_____
_____.

Working Hard to Improve

Here's a trophy for Me!

Hooray for Me!

Name

Vacation Memories

The coolest vacation I ever took was...

To: _____

With: _____

When: _____
Date

Three words that describe the trip are...

☐ Exciting ☐ Relaxing ☐ Lazy ☐ Fun

☐ Peaceful ☐ Awesome ☐ Warm ☐ Busy

☐ _____ ☐ _____ ☐ _____

We stayed in a...

☐ Big Hotel ☐ Tent ☐ Small Motel

☐ Relative's House ☐ Igloo ☐ _____

Some souvenirs I got were...

_____

More Vacation Memories

We traveled by...

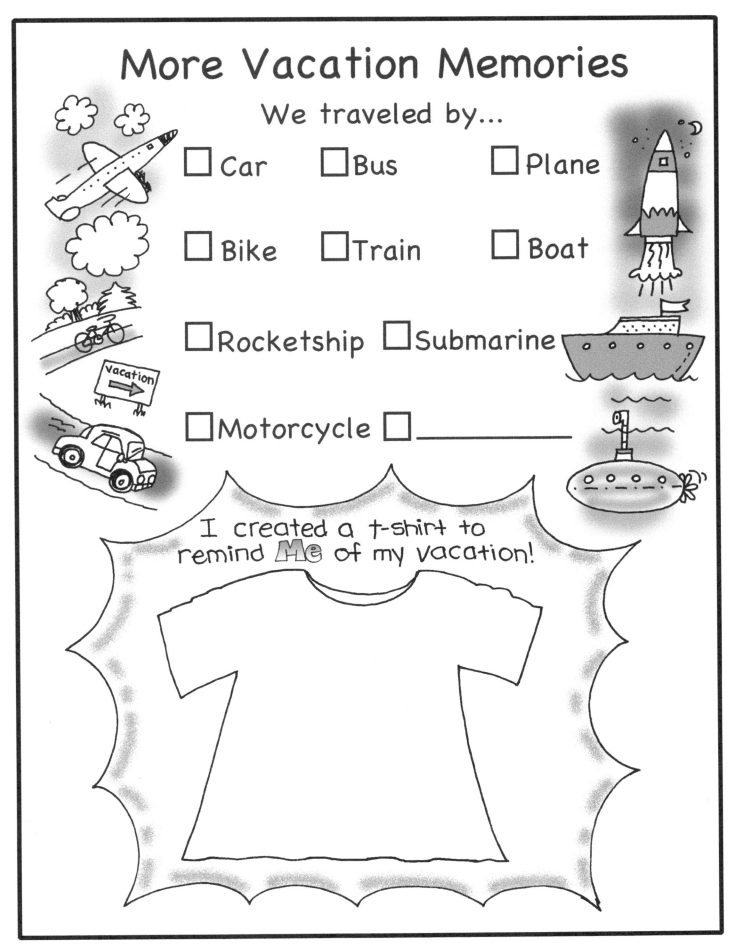

☐ Car   ☐ Bus   ☐ Plane

☐ Bike   ☐ Train   ☐ Boat

☐ Rocketship   ☐ Submarine

☐ Motorcycle   ☐ _____

I created a t-shirt to remind Me of my vacation!

Must Read It!

When it comes to reading, here are my picks...

Favorite Books

_____
_____
_____

Favorite Types of Books

_____

Favorite Authors

_____
_____
_____

Favorite Places to Read

_____
_____

Favorite Characters

_____
_____
_____

Must Watch It! Television

When it comes to TV, here are my picks...

Favorite Shows

_____
_____
_____
_____

Favorite Characters

_____
_____
_____

Favorite Type of Shows

_____
_____

Favorite Times and Places to Watch

_____
_____
_____

Favorite Actors and Actresses

_____
_____
_____

Must Watch It! Movies

When it comes to movies, here are my picks...

Favorite Movies

_____

_____

_____

Favorite Types of Movies

_____

_____

_____

Favorite Characters

_____

_____

_____

Favorite Places to Watch

_____

_____

_____

Favorite Actresses

_____

_____

_____

Favorite Actors

_____

_____

_____

Must Wear It!

When it comes to clothes, here are my picks...

Favorite Type of Clothing _____

My Favorite Style

_____

_____

My Favorite Dress-Up Style

_____

_____

My Favorite Shirt

_____

My Favorite Pants

_____

Favorite Shoes

_____

Favorite Brands

_____

Favorite Clothing Stores

_____

_____

_____

43

More of My Favorites

Gaming System: _____

_____

Games to Play on it:_____

_____

_____

Funny Videos: _____

_____

_____

Websites: _____

_____

_____

Toys I'll Never Tire of:_____

_____

_____

Board Games

I never knew that!

_____

_____

_____

_____

_____

Back in Time

If I could go back in time I'd like to meet and talk to _____

_____

_____

because _____

_____

_____.

I would definitely ask this question:

_____

_____

_____

Time Capsule

If I made a time capsule I'd include...

Interesting Facts About Me in the Year 20___

1.

2.

3.

Interesting "Stuff" I'd Put in it From the Year 20___

_____

_____

Date:

_____

Here's where I'd bury it...

_____

_____

_____

I'd hope someone would find it in ____ years! I think they'd be most surprised to find

_____

_____.

Happy or Sad

Some things that make me smile...

Some things that make me frown...

More About Who I Am

You could call Me...

☐ A Morning Person   ☐ A Night Owl

☐ A T-shirt and Jeans Person   ☐ A Dress-Up Person

☐ A Meat Eater   ☐ A Vegetarian

☐ A Vegan

☐ A Clean Freak   ☐ Kind of Messy

☐ Totally Messy

☐ Artsy   ☐ Sporty   ☐ Bookish

☐ Always Early   ☐ On Time

I got this!

☐ Always Late

Let me think...

Summer Break

I'm hoping this will be my best summer ever!
Here's how I plan to spend it...

World Traveler

If I could go anywhere in the world I'd choose _____
because _____
_____.

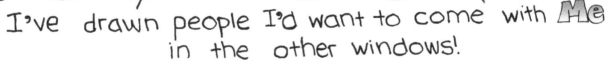

Here's **Me** in the window! I'm on my way!

I've drawn people I'd want to come with **Me** in the other windows!

Leave: _____
Return: _____

← Here's My Plan:

I was Here!
And Here!
And Here, Too!

Circus Life

I'd want to be...

☐ An Acrobat   ☐ A Ringmaster

☐ An Animal Trainer   ☐ A Tightrope Walker

☐ A Clown   ☐ A Trapeze Artist

☐ A Juggler   ☐ A Trampoline Jumper

☐ A Magician   ☐ A Unicycle Rider

Because... _____

_____.

My circus name could be _____.

Picture of Me Performing

Fun, Fun, Fun

Here's a list of some of the things
that I like to do for fun.

Here's a picture of myself on a fun day!

The President and Me

If I could meet with the President of the United States...

I'd like us to meet at _____.

I'd bring _____ with me because _____.

I would wear _____.

I would ask these three questions...

1. _____

_____

2. _____

_____

3. _____

_____

If I could help the president, I'd volunteer to

_____.

Famous Friend

If I could become friends with a famous person, I would choose _____ because _____ _____.

The first place I'd take my famous friend to would be...

☐ My House   ☐ My School   ☐ My Town

☐ _____

The first person I'd introduce my famous friend to would be _____.

If someone took a snapshot of us it'd look like this...

Online Time

I use the Internet to...

☐ Do Schoolwork

☐ Keep in Touch with Friends and Family

☐ Play Games

☐ Learn About Stuff

When using the Internet, I follow these rules:

1. _____

2. _____

3. _____

I spend about _____ hours and _____ minutes online each day.

Sites I would recommend to other kids my age:

* _____

_____

* _____

_____

* _____

I'll have to try these!

Custom Costume

I've designed a costume to wear to a party!

The things I need to make it are _____
_____.

Special touches I could add are _____
_____.

Staying Healthy

Fun ways for Me to exercise are:

☐ Biking ☐ Skating ☐ Walking ☐ Running

☐ Dancing ☐ Swimming ☐ Skate-boarding ☐ Jumping Rope

☐ _____ ☐ _____

Indoor sports I play: _____

Outdoor sports I play: _____

My Exercise Chart

Activity	Mon.	Tues.	Wed.	Thurs.	Fri.	Sat.	Sun.
	___Hrs. ___Mins.	___Hrs. ___Mins.	___Hrs. ___Mins.	___Hrs. ___Mins.	___Hrs. ___Mins.	___Hrs. ___Mins.	___Hrs ___Mins.
	___Hrs. ___Mins.	___Hrs. ___Miins.	___Hrs. ___Mins.	___Hrs. ___Mins.	___Hrs. ___Mins.	___Hrs. ___Mins.	___Hrs. ___Mins.
	___Hrs. ___Mins.	___Hrs. ___Mins.	___Hrs. ___Mins.	___Hrs. ___Mins.	___Hrs. ___Mins.	___Hrs. ___Mins.	___Hrs. ___Mins.

Champion

Nuts About Nature

Where I live...

The coldest month is _____.

The hottest month is _____.

The rainiest month is _____.

My favorite month is _____.

Here's a list of plants, animals, bugs, and birds I've seen in my neighborhood.

Noticing Nature

What I Saw:	Date I Saw it:

Smells Good

I've checked my favorite smells...

☐ Freshly Baked Cookies   ☐ Vanilla

☐ Chocolate   ☐ Baby Lotion

☐ Cinnamon   ☐ Fresh Laundry

☐ Freshly Cut Grass   ☐ Bacon

☐ Peppermint   ☐ Coconut

☐ _____   ☐ _____

If I could create a new candle scent it'd be

_____.

I don't think I would ever get tired of the smell of _____ _____.

M-m-m-m-m-m-m

My Recipe for Happiness

There are many "ingredients" that make up a happy life. Here is my recipe using the ones I feel are most important.

Faith Laughter Hope

Understanding Sunshine Thoughtfulness

Patience Peace

Love Wisdom

Kindness Exercise

Healthy Food

Money Energy

Recipe

3 Cups _____
1 1/2 Cups _____
1/2 Cup _____
1/4 Cup _____
2 Tablespoons _____
1 Teaspoon _____
A Dash of _____

Mix together well... And enjoy!

Talent Fresh Air

Luck Positive Thinking

Good Health Friendship

Happily Ever After

In 20 years I think I will be...

_____

_____

_____

_____

_____

_____

_____

_____

_____

_____

It will be fun to look back someday and see how things turned out!

Filling Up This Journal...

☐ Was Fun

☐ Made Me Think

☐ Makes Me Want to Keep Writing

Good-bye!